Quaestiones Perversas

Beatriz E. Balanta &
Mary Walling Blackburn

Pioneer Works Press

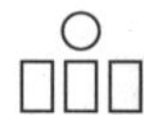

Contents

Beautiful Economy

ARE: ANHOEK RECORD EXAMINATION

SUBJECT AREA

BEAUTIFUL ECONOMY

—

Verbal Section

ANTONYM

1. New

(A) newe
(B) neowe
(C) niewe
(D) niew
(E) ald

2. Beautiful

(A) be(a)ute
(B) belte
(C) ~~grace~~
(D) bell(us)
(E) beltet

3. Economy

(A) oikonomia
(B) beauty
(C) house + nomia
(D) house + management
(E) thrifty management

4. Longing

- (A) hoping
- (B) lacking
- (C) waiting
- (D) needing
- (E) coolness

5. the Absence of Something

- (A) something missing
- (B) something missed
- (C) something lacking
- (D) innovation
- (E) some lack

6. Innovation

- (A) fresh
- (B) weird
- (C) viral
- (D) stillness
- (E) new

7. Invention

- (A) found
- (B) founder
- (C) foundling
- (D) fondling
- (E) flirting

8. RECESSION : INVENTION

- (A) free love : exploitation
- (B) gesture : Taylorism
- (C) depression : lull
- (D) finicky : democracy
- (E) flood : fertilization

9. CONSUMPTION : GEOPHAGIA

- (A) Pornography : NAMBLA
- (B) nanotechnology : contamination
- (C) car accident : organ donation
- (D) Basement Dweller : Bower Bird
- (E) longing : anorexia

10. REGULATION : INNOVATION
PERVERSION : COMMODITY

- (A) Bureau of Indian Affairs : reservation casino
- (B) anti-abortion legislation : wild carrot as aborteffiecient (1 Tablespoon per day)
- (C) canceled bus route : rogue urban passenger vans (consult crypto-timetables)
- (D) drug enforcement : anti-snitch multi-media DVDs produced by drug dealers
- (E) Victorian cadaver trade deficit : poorhouse healthcare in lieu of future exchange of corpse

11. The prisoner's weapons were confiscated by the guards and handed over to ________________.

Ⓐ their children
Ⓑ their superiors
Ⓒ the museum
Ⓓ eBay
Ⓔ the waste facility

12. The design of the inmate's homemade shank was ________________ but persuasive.

Ⓐ beautiful
Ⓑ copied
Ⓒ invented
Ⓓ crude
Ⓔ resourceful

13. Despite a renewed interest in sustainability, prisoners' inventions were ________________ only in relationship to their subscribed circumstances, and at release prisoners were not hired by innovation think tanks or sustainable design firms.

Ⓐ coveted
Ⓑ distributed
Ⓒ adopted
Ⓓ aesthetisized
Ⓔ innovative

14. Immigration Detention is perceived as the next market for the Corrections Corporation of America (CCA), a private prison corporation who was a key architect and proponent of SB1070, a law which

- (A) makes "attrition through enforcement the public policy of all state and local government agencies in Arizona."
- (B) allows for the transfer of detained immigrants to facilities that capitalize on their labor.
- (C) stipulates that a person is not eligible for suspension or commutation of sentence or release on any basis until the sentence imposed is served, which guarantees their labor in the service of the companies who contract for prisoner labor.
- (D) is the strictest and broadest anti-immigration law passed in US history.
- (E) All of the above

15. Economic innovation is not solely the production and dissemination of invention; the manner in which the entrepreneurial spirit harnesses existing resources (legal, corporal, federal) in new ways can also be framed as innovation. Several of the 37 states and 4 county-based certified ________________ industry programs offer Prison Blues line of denim clothing, Hard Timin Relaxed Fit Protective StabVest, and Big House Choppers which includes a model entitled "The Shank" ($48,900), for consumer purchase.

- (A) vocational
- (B) correctional
- (C) apparel
- (D) heavy
- (E) light

16. The Consumer hesitates to purchase and wear a 14 ounce 100% cotton denim skirt featuring a heavy duty brass zipper with metal button closure and five riveted reinforced pockets. A "Hard Timin" logo is sewn onto the exterior of some garments, because it is the label for this particular brand of clothing made by US prisoners. The Consumer hesitates because

_______________.

- (A) the Consumer fears the perception that the garment is worn with irony.
- (B) the Consumer never purchases clothing online.
- (C) the Consumer refuses to support the prison industrial complex.
- (D) the Consumer is concerned with seasonal trends and/or name brand recognition.
- (E) the Consumer does not know the specific crime of the individual machine operator who has touched the denim that will be worn against the body.

17. The Capitalist did not refer to her economy as a "Beautiful Economy" because the structure was beautiful, the _______________ were.

- Ⓐ fantasies
- Ⓑ fetish objects
- Ⓒ possessions
- Ⓓ prizes
- Ⓔ competitions

18. An object that exists within one socio-economic structure, and emerges within another socio-economic system, must invent a ________________ to support its migration.

- Ⓐ psychological desire
- Ⓑ fetish economy
- Ⓒ rubric for seduction
- Ⓓ military application
- Ⓔ bullshit lifestyle campaign

19. The Capitalist conceived of the objects he interacted with as his possessions, but the Communist conceived of the objects she interacted with as her ________________.

- Ⓐ siblings
- Ⓑ enemies
- Ⓒ gods
- Ⓓ children
- Ⓔ comrades

20. The Citizen wondered: If we refuse the capitalist framing of object as something we possess AND we reject the communist framing that the object is our

friend, could we devise a radically divergent socio-economic structure that was contingent on any object that touched us as being perceived as a ________________?

- (A) an ancestor
- (B) robot
- (C) cannibal
- (D) alien
- (E) sermon

EXCERPT FROM TEXT BY WRITER, PHILOSOPHER AND ACTIVIST GUY HOCQUENGHEM

Ants do not have abortions. Ants are not homosexual. Ants do not draft wills. Ants do not travel to the moon. Ants do not play football and do not play on Wall Street. Ants are natural. With the human machine, it's the opposite. We can read our conditions most legibly in those areas that are the farthest removed from our conditioning, those zones between order and desire where the string of injury is the greatest and the callus covering the wound is most developed.

21. Which of the following titles best describes the content of the passage as a whole:

- (A) The Post-Traumatic Cyborg: A Diagnosis
- (B) Queen Right: Understanding Sapiens Through Mycocepurus
- (C) A Sociopolitical Mapping of Interstitial Emotions
- (D) The Condition of the French Christian Right
- (E) None of the Above

22. According to Hocquenghem, the human machine:

- (A) does not have abortions
- (B) is not homosexual
- (C) differentiates itself via trauma
- (D) does not travel to the moon

Ⓔ does not play football and does not play on Wall Street

23. It can be inferred from the text that that the term natural:

Ⓐ is not categorically good
Ⓑ includes human machines
Ⓒ is a construct that shifts according to use value
Ⓓ excludes the moon
Ⓔ is used to partition that which is unnatural

EXCERPT FROM SCIENCE FICTION WRITER URSULA K. LE GUIN'S PERSONAL BLOG

This is not an acceptable use of the word. "Technology" and "hi tech" are not synonymous, and a technology that isn't "hi," isn't necessarily "low" in any meaningful sense.

We have been so desensitized by a hundred and fifty years of ceaselessly expanding technical prowess that we think nothing less complex and showy than a computer or a jet bomber deserves to be called "technology" at all. As if linen were the same thing as flax—as if paper, ink, wheels, knives, clocks, chairs, aspirin pills, were natural objects, born with us like our teeth and fingers—as if steel saucepans with copper bottoms and fleece vests spun from recycled glass grew on trees, and we just picked them when they were ripe...One way to illustrate that most technologies are, in fact, pretty "hi," is to ask yourself of any manmade object, Do I know how to make one?

Anybody who ever lighted a fire without matches has probably gained some proper respect for "low" or "primitive" or "simple" technologies; anybody who ever lighted a fire with matches should have the wits to respect that notable hi-tech invention.

I don't know how to build and power a refrigerator, or program a computer, but I don't know how to make a fishhook or a pair of shoes, either. I could learn. We all can learn. That's the neat thing about technologies. They're what we can learn to do.

And all science fiction is, in one way or another, technological. Even when it's written by people who don't know what the word means.

All the same, I agree with my reviewer that I don't write hard science fiction. Maybe I write easy science fiction. Or maybe the hard stuff's inside, hidden—like bones, as opposed to an exoskeleton...

24. Please remember these lines after the test has long come to a close:

Ⓐ As if linen were the same thing as flax—
Ⓑ as if paper, ink, wheels, knives, clocks, chairs, aspirin pills, were natural objects,
Ⓒ born with us like our teeth and fingers
Ⓓ as if steel saucepans with copper bottoms and fleece vests spun from recycled glass
Ⓔ and we just picked them when they were ripe...

25. One way to illustrate that most technologies are, in fact, pretty "hi," is to ask yourself of any manmade object:

Ⓐ Do I know how to make one?
Ⓑ Do I know how to make?
Ⓒ Do I know how to?
Ⓓ Do I know how?
Ⓔ Do I know?

AN EXCERPT FROM AN ORAL HISTORY FIELD RECORDING INTERVIEW WITH KATSI COOK: MOHAWK MIDWIFE AND ENVIRONMENTAL ACTIVIST

When you research the literature, you'll find in the last 50, 30 years, that the biggest technology we have to improve maternal and child health outcomes is not the ultrasound machine or a drug or some hightech machine that costs a lot of money, it's simply being in the room with the woman as she's laboring. It's simply going to the woman's home and reassuring her and talking with her. And that's what a doula does. You get a doula to follow a course of care from beginning to end. And end is when? In our community, it never ends. You attach to that child-and-mother pair, and you're always there as a consultant to them, and as a friend—and in my case, a cousin in the extended family. I love it. You know, that's the difference between me and a certified nurse midwife. A certified nurse midwife that delivered my grandson, I've known [her] for years, but I noticed in her scope of practice, she gets to do the delivery, but the minute that boy is out he is handed over to a pediatrician. The continuity is broken. And unless I make a special effort, she'll never see that boy again. I think that's a crime, because she's part of his birth story. She belongs in his life. But because it's a highly technological biomedical construct, she's out of his life unless we make an effort. And so, what I'm talking about brings together some of what we know from social constructs, from the new science of complexity. We know that the most powerful technology we have as human beings is how we get along, how we're biologically programmed to be with one another. And so, doulas are part of that.

26. The technologies utilized for your own birth included:

- (A) Midwife and/or Doula
- (B) Cesarean section
- (C) Epidural Block for pain
- (D) Diethylstilbestrol (a synthetic nonsteroidal estrogen given to pregnant women in the mistaken belief it would reduce the risk of pregnancy complications and losses (1940–1970). In 1971, DES was shown to cause a rare vaginal tumor in girls and women who had been exposed to this drug in utero.
- (E) Postnatal Glucocorticoid or dexamethasone therapy for lung disease of prematurity.

27. The excerpt cannot contain the entire interview. It is likely that Cook may have also explained:

- (A) that the bark of the wild cherry tree is a COX-2 enzyme inhibitor, just like Celebrex, Vioxx, and Bextra, but does not cause heart attacks when ingested as a tea.
- (B) that the Mohawk word for vulva is “nice canoe” and that it defuses misogyny because it cannot be uttered with fury or disgust.
- (C) that massaging the laboring woman’s breasts increases the frequency of the contractions.
- (D) at the Loon Lake Conference [where traditional chiefs, clan mothers, and young activists from the Six Nations worked to

define sovereignty for Native peoples; they identified control of reproduction as one of its essential elements]: "You know, here's all these hippies and they get along well enough that they have all these institutions. They decided how they were going to do it on their own. Why can't we learn from that?"

- (E) that the cervix dilates in labor when the partner of the woman giving birth tells her "I love you."

28. After reading Cook do you:

- (A) seek out the person who delivered you in order to re-enlist a continuity deferred?
- (B) seek to consult with, to be friends with a woman who is about to give birth and to assist in the process as a form of community as technology? Do you know how? Is this beautiful economy?
- (C) wonder if Cook would ascertain that it is, in fact, a technological breakdown when a child and its deliverer never speak to one another again after birth?
- (D) begin to think of all your frayed intimacies as technological breakdowns? Could a community (of human machines) repair the ruptures generated by individual human machines without exhaustion of resources?
- (E) fear the implied moral imperative of engaging, when birthing sometimes includes death?

END OF MULTIPLE CHOICE QUESTIONS

Please select two questions (1–28) from two discrete categories. For example, if one question is in the Analogy section, the other selected question must be in the Reading Comprehension, Antonym, or Sentence Completion section. Both selected questions cannot share the same category.

Please explain the logic of your answer. Use diagrams, outlines, or lists if necessary.

Repeat same process with second selection.

Please use the additional booklet provided to write your essay. Be sure to include the number of the question and your answer within your response.

The Reproductive

ARE: ANHOEK RECORD EXAMINATION

SUBJECT AREA

THE REPRODUCTIVE

—

Verbal Section

1. The schoolyard is the grounds of ritual utterances; a prescribed oath binds the child to their juvenile community. Select one:

I, ________________, swear:

- (A) May the floor open / If I have an untrue word spoken.
- (B) Wet my thumb / Wipe it dry / Cut my throat / If I tell a lie.
- (C) Pinky, pinky, bow-bell / Whoever tells a lie / Will sink down to a bad place / And never rise up again.
- (D) Here's the Bible open / Here's the Bible shut / If I do not tell the truth / I hope me throat is cut.
- (E) Little pig, little pig, tell me a lie / And I'll knock the fat clean out of your eye.

2. [illegible]

- (A) [illegible]
- (B) [illegible]
- (C) [illegible]

3. riprədəktɪv

- (A) mek ə kapi
- (B) ækt əv fɔrmɪŋ əgɛn
- (C) bɪkəm prɛgnənt
- (D) dəstrɔj ðə fərtɪləti əv

4. Reproductive

- (A) Make a copy
- (B) Act in forming again
- (C) To cause to multiply
- (D) Destroy the beginning
- (E) Start over (stutter)

4. Child

- (A) twig
- (B) puppet
- (C) beast
- (D) clone
- (E) All of the above

5. Child

(A) young thief
(B) young animal
(C) carrion
(D) infant
(E) none of the above

6. Fetus

(A) ghost fruit
(B) honeycomb
(C) fiddlehead
(D) bubbling code
(E) rawest data

7. Woman

(A) bubbling code
(B′) rawest data
(C) none of the above
(D) none below
(E) wif

8. FETUS : CRUCIFIX

- (A) meadow : football stadium
- (B) pedestrian : handcuffs of the campus security office
- (C) congress : lipstick stain
- (D) scintilla : telescope
- (E) sulfur : car

9. STATE : BREAST

- (A) secret : thumb Drive
- (B) memoir : ghostwriter
- (C) Apple : rare earth
- (D) cock : leafblower
- (E) animalcule : animal

10. CITY OF WOMEN : REPUBLIC OF CHILDREN

- (A) 21st century prisoners' abortion rights : Mothering from Inside
- (B) 19th century British Female Insane Asylum as Holding Tank for Unruly Middle Class Wives : control classroom for child dosages of ritalin administered to establish inhibitory control
- (C) the Women's Encampment for a Future of Peace and Justice : the Seneca White Deer of the Seneca Army Depot
- (D) Some of the above

Ⓔ None of the above

11. HOME : BIRTH

Ⓐ bride catalog : a nephew's choice
Ⓑ codes of reproductive vaginal intercourse : race
Ⓒ knowledge : shaker furniture
Ⓓ consent : to not be a single being
Ⓔ waves : waves

12. ISIS : Isis

Ⓐ Liberté : stigmata
Ⓑ free bleed : surface tension
Ⓒ rainbow : Magna Carta
Ⓓ airborne ashes : afterbirth
Ⓔ diethylstilbestrol : hope

13. (see image 1) : (see image 2)

Ⓐ exorcism : family reunion
Ⓑ gesture : remote control
Ⓒ poetry : pyramid
Ⓓ Alien : Predator
Ⓔ Orgasm : Organism

14. According to some legal scholars, child pornography law unequivocally demands the viewer to reproduce ________________ in order to suss out pictures of children that harbor secret pedophilic appeal.

- (A) the gaze of the pedophile
- (B) the cock of the cop
- (C) the hole of the photograph
- (D) a robot's algorithm
- (E) none of the above

15. Question the paradox of fetal motherhood, which always peaks at wartime. Study "the bump" as it appears in mechanical reproduction (tabloid press) in order to establish the hidden sexual charge of pregnancy. Which question lingers in relation?

- (A) Is this a still of a starlet derived from a psychoanalytic snuff film that ends in the death of the ego? Or is this publicity shot of doubled star a celebration of two citizens in one?
- (B) How is the libido entangled in the fetus (i.e. The Tom Cruise Effect)?
- (C) Why would reproduction reproduce desire (i.e. The Beyonce Effect)?
- (D) When does the status of the mother follow the status of the fetus (i.e. Princess Kate effect)?

(E) Can you extract the fact of a pregnancy from motherhood as ending (i.e. The Marilyn Monroe Effect)?

16. Robert Wyman, professor of Molecular, Cellular, and Developmental Biology at Yale, frames population growth as a measurable driver of human and environmental misery. Additionally, Wyman refers to ________________ as an effect of unequal reproductive possibility amongst primates (human and otherwise).

(A) patriarchy as expressed through the "Beta Male" serial killer
(B) the act of an orangutan raping a human who served as the cook at a biologist's encampment
(C) subordinate sexually frustrated male gorillas murdering the offspring of their rivals
(D) Dr. Cecil Jacobson's surreptitious use of his own sperm (rather than that of the agreed upon donor) to inseminate 15-75 clients at his fertility clinic
(E) B and C

17. "The guerillas don't ________________. They eat, when they can, but they don't ________________. They have important things to do, things that require all their energy." (Dana Densmore, "On Celibacy," 1968)

(A) screw, screw
(B) talk, consent

Ⓒ come, make each other come
Ⓓ procreate, procreate
Ⓔ exist, exist

Wall Text
(Norman Wait Harris Purchase Fund, 2006. 68):

It's a New Age
Sue Williams
American, born 1954
Acrylic and oil on canvas

Williams's darkly sarcastic caricature paintings address difficult topics such as domestic violence, rape, pornography, and misogyny. In early paintings like "It's a New Age," characteristic scrawls, doodles, erasures, graphic representations of the body, and text convey the artist's own scathingly critical thoughts. Her voice, which takes the form of transcribed, seemingly unedited notes, asserts her identity as both a woman and a painter. Williams uses verbal puns and scatological imagery to comment on the degradation of the female body through sexual violence and abuse and on the psychological trauma of self-loathing. The artist parodies the politics of "choice"—she declares in the painting she is "free to choose" and "I chose fat thighs"—by articulating personal struggle.

18. The artist is best described as:

- (A) A woman
- (B) Both a woman and a painter
- (C) A painter
- (D) An articulator or articulation of personal struggle

19. “The artist parodies the politics of ‘choice’”:

- (A) by declaring in the painting she is “free to choose”
- (B) by declaring “I chose fat thighs”
- (C) by declaring she is free to choose and I chose fat thighs
- (D) by articulating personal struggle

20. Which of the following would make the most logical sense as an addition to the above passage:

- (A) That floating lizard fetus with a beak on the left hand side?
- (B) No, not a lizard, the painting says: “a human fetus, or is it still in its chicken stage”?
- (C) stating “the ass grows hard-to-reach tufts—another odd choice, perhaps my mind was elsewhere”?
- (D) let us get back to that fetus—“maybe a little afraid”?
- (E) or, is it still in its chicken stage?

EXCERPTS FROM A TEXT BY WRITER AND ACTIVIST SHULAMITH FIRESTONE

Present oral contraception is at only a primitive (faulty) stage, only one of many types of fertility control now under experiment. Artificial insemination and artificial inovulation are already a reality. Choice of sex of the fetus, test-tube fertilization...are just around the corner. Several teams of scientists are working on the development of an artificial placenta. Even parthenogenesis—virgin birth—could be developed very soon.

Are people, even scientists, themselves, culturally prepared for any of this? Decidedly not. A recent Harris poll, quoted in Life magazine, representing a broad sampling of Americans—including, for example, Iowa farmers—found a surprising number willing to consider the new methods. The hitch was that they would consider them only where they reinforced and furthered present values of family life and reproduction, e.g., to help a barren woman have her husband's child. Any question that could be interpreted as a furthering of liberation per se was rejected flatly as unnatural. But note that it was not the "test-tube" baby itself that was thought unnatural...but the new value system, based on the elimination of male supremacy and the family.

...Fears of new methods of reproduction are so widespread that as of the time of this writing, 1969, the subject, outside of scientific circles, is still taboo. Even many women in the women's liberation movement...are afraid to express any interest in it for fear of confirming the suspicion that they are "unnatural."...Let me then say it bluntly: Pregnancy is barbaric...Pregnancy is the temporary deformation of the body of the individual for the sake of the species.

Moreover, childbirth hurts. And it isn't good for you. Three thousand years ago, women giving birth "naturally" had no need to pretend that pregnancy was a real trip, some mystical orgasm (that far-away look). The Bible said it: pain and travail...And after it was over, even during it, they were admired in a limited way for their bravery; their valor was measured by how many children (sons) they could endure bringing to the world.

21. It can be inferred from the text that Firestone believes that Iowa farmers:

- (A) possess outsize importance in national polls, due to the schedule of American presidential primary elections.
- (B) are unusually accepting of artificial insemination, due to their experiences with animal husbandry.
- (C) have particularly acute knowledge of the brute nature of reproduction, due to their experiences with animal husbandry.
- (D) are of a hardy stock, due to the barren winters.
- (E) represent a highly conservative strain of American patriarchy.

22. According to Firestone, the possibility of parthenogenesis would:

- (A) herald a new value system
- (B) be anti-Biblical

- (C) rob women of a mystical experience
- (D) usher in societal liberation
- (E) be anti-orgasmic

23. Which of the following synonyms could be substituted in the above text for the word valor:

- (A) Fearlessness
- (B) Tenacity
- (C) Stomach
- (D) Intestinal fortitude
- (E) Indomitableness

24. Identify the original and terminal points of the pictured life cycle (select all possible answers):
[SEE IMAGE 3]

- (A) Fertilized egg and adult medusa
- (B) Larva and polyp
- (C) Polyp and adult medusa
- (D) Polyp transforming and Adult Medusa
- (E) None of the above
- (F) Mouth
- (G) Feeding arm
- (H) Young medusa
- (I) Jelly

25. Listen to the two song pairs provided. Write while listening. Discuss musical features of each work (form, instrumentation, melody, etc.). Speculate on the songwriter's intent and their positioning of the song in relation to the politics of their time. Locate and discuss submerged or metanarratives within the song that may run counter to this intent. Imagine all four songs combined into a single song; describe the sonic, affective and ideological content of this song.

26. Read the following account from a full-spectrum doula (one who works with birth, abortion, adoption, surrogacy, miscarriage and stillbirth.) Write one punctuation mark, extinct or common, in response.

F|Slash|F Marks

F|SLASH|F MARKS SAMPLE TEST

F|SLASH|F MARKS SAMPLE TEST PEER EVALUATION

—

Is this test acceptable to the professional community of feminists and other testers? Is there a need for a new test?

1. To pie or to cream the public female, to instigate "cream psychosis" (Georges Le Gloupier) flows against and with and through an ingrained aversion to Woman when:

- (A) Marguerite Duras' face is unrecognizable sheathed in chocolate icing. She is cake-clobbered by Georges Le Gloupier (1969) because "she has a kind of intelligence and cleverness that serves only her own vanity."
- (B) a suddenly featureless (creamed) (and clothed) Linda Lovelace creampies her *Deep Throat* co-stars in a sunlit parking lot (1972).
- (C) former Pie Kill Unlimited Aron Kay smashes an apple pie in the face of ERA opponent Phyllis Schlafly at the National Republican Women's Club Luncheon (1977).
- (D) Anita Bryant, a former beauty queen, homophobe and Florida citrus representative, working to repeal anti-discriminatory legislation on a national level, is pied by Thom L. Higgins, gay-rights activist (1977). It is strawberry-rhubarb; Bryant puns about its "fruit."
- (E) None operate as this question claims. Tester, I pie you. Funeral Pie, you. Female pie you. All people pied here are females. I sexed you and you are female. (The filling for a funeral pie, an American regional dish prepared for wakes, is raisin or sour cherry.)

2. Which feminine marks mark feminist marks, Mark?

(A) Althusser's mother points to the child's feminine trace, a cream leak, the sheet holding a nocturnal emission. Housed in that Oedipal moment, she claims the future philosopher is now a man; the future man claims the pointing finger slashes at his phallus. Which one? (Althusser, pied-noir, 1931, one year after leaving Algeria for Marseilles). Is there a subset of gender assignations for colonists as burnished by colonialism?

A. Monique Wittig: I am not a writer, I am a lesbian.
B. Jeanette Winterson: I am not a lesbian who happens to write.
C. Marguerite Young: I am not a woman, I am a writer.
D. Theresa Hyuk Cha: I write. I write you. Daily. From here.
E. Hilda Hilst: It's not a book—it's a banana.
F. Pauline Oliveros: Maybe we need banana-shaped ears.

3. Which category holds?
   (A) (C) (D) (E) (F)
4. Which category holds us?
   (A) (C) (D) (E) (F)
5. Which category holds meusthemmeme?
   (A) (C) (D) (E) (F)
6. Which category holds the academic ones?
   (A) (C) (D) (E) (F)
7. Which category holds the gross ones?
   (A) (C) (D) (E) (F)
8. Which category holds the licked one, wet and drying?
   (A) (C) (D) (E) (F)
9. Which category holds gender over the empty elevator shaft, cold air rushing up?
   (A) (C) (D) (E) (F)

10. How badly are you feeling?

- Ⓐ You feel unsafe.
- Ⓑ You feel unglued.
- Ⓒ Me feel unglued.
- Ⓓ Me feel the death drive.
- Ⓔ Let's cease now.

11. Have you thought of slashing

- Ⓐ the you that is she who suckles (femina)?
- Ⓑ what is otherwise referred to as the feminine self?
- Ⓒ the feminist self?
- Ⓓ all selves?
- Ⓔ a rubber mountain-bike tire open, not as Carol Rama does (for sculpture), but to make a belt for your pants?

12. Feminine Visual Arrangement : Safety

Ⓐ Her bare child back in photograph (it curves) (Boston, 1917) : her *postural deformity*. (To order numbers without damage is possible.) Documented by the social photographer (Lewis Hine) as evidence of unsafe work conditions for child bookkeepers.

Ⓑ She strokes her gray beard : Circus boxcar ("Lady Olga" 1871–1951 (synthetic title | true 13 inch beard;| alloyed genealogy|the Real Jane's nucleotides named: Catawba/Irish/ Jewish)

Ⓒ Water tumbler balanced on the cult figure née speed junkie née mother head, her head : her fellow telepathe, speed junkie nee *ugly spirit* née writer guides the bullet into her skull, with her, or despite her. A forensics of their psychic communique? (Mexico City, 1951), Joan Vollmer & William Burroughs had a parlour trick called William Tell. Tester, If you had an extra life to spare, you'd try it, too.

Ⓓ Saloon Girl re-enactment sepia-tone photograph (1980) : Sex-worker holograms (2030)

Ⓔ Poly-satin crotch : Candida Albicans

Ⓕ The palms of Karen Wood's mittens were white : Donald Rogerson mistook Karen for a white-tailed deer (Bangor 1988.) KW was pinning laundry to the line in her backyard.

Rogerson: 'I've shot a human being! Oh God! Why does God allow this to happen?"

(an initial psychiatric intake is passing through THE EXAM)

13. Have you wanted to die

- (A) in a feminine manner?
- (B) as a feminist?
- (C) because of the feminine?
- (D) because the feminine and the feminist were untangled and all past was estranged?
- (E) because the femme owned feminism again and all the present was estranged?

14. Have you tried to kill

- (A) the feminine?
- (B) the feminist?
- (C) the suckling self?
- (D) My Mother Man; His Evil Nurse; lesser avatar School Secretary: Agent Provocateur for the Phallus...people sexed female and yes, with authoritarian tongues and hands?

15. If not, what held you back?

- (A) I imagined the crime-scene photographs. My leg that is no longer my leg. I imagined melodrama. A laser-cut grave.
- (B) Astronomical twilight doubles down each

day, holding a body away from other bodies and holding a body towards itself, towards night absorbed then day absorbed then night absorbed again. It is the timed sensation of non-creaturely dissolution that absolves… something.

INTERRUPTION

THE APOCALYPSE WILL COME AND GO AND COME.

THERE WILL BE NO SUBJECT AREA RECORD
OF YOUR STRENGTHS AND INTEREST,
IN FEMININE MARKS AND/OR FEMINIST MARKS,
IN MANEEN MARKS OR BY PENIS TRACK.

ME TESTER, MY GOLD CROWNS HAVE
BEEN MELTED DOWN. ME NO I.
ME SON, WE WON'T PREPARE SON FOR
A TEST THAT NEVER WILL BE.
ME UNTESTED SON AND GROLAR BEAR
DRINK THE FINAL WATER

THERE NEVER WAS A SUBJECT AREA TEST BECAUSE
THERE NEVER WAS ANY FUNDING. THERE NEVER
WAS A CORPORATION THAT WANTED TO EVALUATE
AN APPLICANT'S' DISAVOWAL OF GENDER.

CONTENT SPECIFICATIONS

Sonic scope of the test includes materials below. Percentage of the score follows.

Joan Armatrading: *Me, Myself, I* (1980) Video	1%
The Bags (Los Angeles): *We Will Bury You* (1983)	1%
Connie Converse: *The Witch and the Wizard* (1954)	1%
Betty Davis: *He Was a Big Freak* (1974)	1%
Lizzy Mercier Descloux: *Herpes Simplex* (1978–1999)	1%
Marianne Faithfull and Ziggy Stardust: *I Got You Babe.* Cover. Live performance (October 19, 1973) Video	1%
Fancy Rosy: *Punk Police* (1977)	1%
Fred Smith: *Talking Wheelchair Blues* (1984)	1%
Serge Gainsbourg: *Lemon Incest* (1984)	1%
Jobriath: I'maman (1974)	1%
Eartha Kitt: *I Love Men*, Metronome Germany (1984) Video	2%

Ms. Krazie: *Baby, I'm Not for Real*	2%
NBJ: *Dead Porker* (1982)	2%
New Haven's Women's Liberation Band: *Shotgun* (1972)	3%
Evelyn Nesbit: *Because I'm No Man's Woman Now* (1930)	4%
Oh Blimey: *Bassface* (2014) Video	4%
Princess Buster: *Ten Commandments to a Man* (1967)	4%
Smoke: *Fatherland* (1995) Humanland	4%
Queen Key: *Calling All Eaters* (2016)	5%
Cha(b)vela Vargas: *La Llorona* (1990)	5%
Yoko Ono: *Yes, I'm a Witch!* (1974)	5%

Visual/cultural nodes of the test follows the distribution below.

Ángeles arcobuceros (17th century Peru and Bolivia)	1%
Arunachalam Muruganantham blood industry	1%
Trưng Sisters' armour in and out of pregnancy (40 AD)	1%
Boxcar Bertha: *Sister of the Road* (1937)	1%
Lynda Benglis: *The Amazing Bow Wow* (1976)	1%
John Gutzon de la Mothe Borglum, sculptor of Mt. Rushmore and KKK member. Note controversy regarding the gender of angels carved for St. John the Divine	1%
Janet Frame: *Sister Buffalo* (1972)	2%
Patricia Johanson: *Delta Duck Potato* (1985) at Leonhardt Lagoon, Dallas, Texas	2%
Adrienne Kennedy: *A Lesson in Dead Language* (1964)	2%
Adrienne Kennedy's Movie Star Scrapbook (1943–1946)	2%
Bhanu Kapil: *Schizophrene* (2011)	3%

Jennifer Gibbons: *Discomania* (undated)	3%
Harlem's Lafargue Clinic (1946–1981) "Observation of Children Watching *Cinderella* (1955)"	3%
Lumber Camp Lady (carved figures used in 19th century midwest lumber camps)	4%
The Modern School at Stelton, New Jersey (1914–1958) Anarchist Primary Education	4%
Grisélidis Réal (Anarchist-Whore): *Prison Journal*	4%
Mount Tamalpais as marking & marked by Etel Adnan, Arthur Russell, Anna Halprin, Cookie Mueller	5%
Hannah Wilke's laser cut gravestone	5%
Dinah Young: *Roadside Grave* (1990s)	5%

SAMPLE TEST PEER EVALUATION

Is this test acceptable to the professional community of feminists and other testers? Is there a need for a new test?

INDEPENDENT EVALUATOR RESPONSE

Is the mark transformative?
When does the mark become a scar? a brand? a slash? a sign? a structure?
Can we ever slash the mark? Why would we want to do that?
Is the mark genetic?
In here the act of pieing seems to be a sign of opposition, protest, it signals profound disagreement...Pieing is an act of humiliation...Pieing is most effective when the pie lands on somebody's face. This act shames and humiliates the culprit. But why the focus on the face? Is staining someone's face a politic act? Can humiliation be garnered as a political strategy? When and where?

Cream pies are generally white. Interesting because the whiteness of the pie dirties the culprit, the accused.
Since when is white a thing/substance that stains and marks? White is usually the substance that is stained...not the staining substance.

Barthes is no feminist. But in his famous book, he longs for the picture of his deceased mother as child. A mother that ultimately refuses to appear photographically. In her stead, we get photographs of Black subjects. Photographs through which he develops his theory of the punctum, the thing in the photograph, that leaps out and cuts us. Why is his mother in-visible? Why is she replaced with black subjects subject to the camera? Is his mother black? or is he actively trying to birth Black people?

In the early '50s Josephine Baker adopted 10 boys and 2 girls from different countries, including Japan, Ghana, and Venezuela. Her project: to become the mother who cancels out différance.

Madame Satã: A boy who became a mare (his mother marked him as such when she exchanged him for the four-legged animal). He then chose to mark/masque his being as a female version of Satan. How deep are his marks?

Marceline Baldwin:...wife of Jim Jones...the infamous cult leader who took death to Guyana...Together they adopted part-Native American child named Agnes, three Korean children, Stephanie, Lew and Suzanne, and in 1961 were the first white couple in Indianapolis to adopt a black child, a boy they named James Warren Jones, Jr.

Is this a form of maddened feminism?

Can we mark the one who chooses to be feminine as a feminist? Here I am thinking of transgender women who in their drive to the feminine mark/slash/transform their body to assume the position of the oppressed. Is this a political act?

Have you wanted to die because you're the only
one who holds the magic of reproduction?

Have you wanted to die because for you
there is no feminine mystic?

Have you wanted to die because you ain't a woman?

Have you wanted to die because you gave
birth to the mongrel race?

Have you wanted to die because the cream that fills you
up marks you as a (non)subject of enjoyment?

Doggy Doggy

ALL: ANHOEK LISTENING LAB

(DOGGY) MOUTH OF (DOGGY) TRUTH LANGUAGE LAB

—

Headphones on.

Listen to the following mixed-up sentences and rearrange towards sense making.

Suck'n, Great Dick, Fancy, Fatt'n, Ball and Vinegar Tom -in witch trials- Because the animal is elided with the female body In Melampronea (1681): suckling from moles/warts/polyps. siphoned human blood from the witches' teats, The dogs, cats, mice, rabbits, bees recorded by name-

riding dogs. in dream like states According to Inquisitorial archive, the peasants torture- fragmented testimony included professional anti-witches,

leaves his body in the form of a small animal but later finds himself to be a peasant fighting for survival against skilled interrogators whose purpose is never entirely clear. The Good Rider, a peasant counter-witch who wears his caul around his neck, in order to enter the Night Battle.

urged to make and bake and fake out of rye meal mixed with the urine of the afflicted girls Tituba and John Indian, the reverend's slaves, were in hopes that when fed to the dog the spell would force the canine familiar to reveal the sorcerer. a traditional english witchcake

Respond to the question or the command after the bell rings:

1. The witchfinder, a professional anti-witch, wets his practice with early capitalism.
What determines the price of killing a witch and her dog?
(Answer: Executioner, hemp, witch-finder.)

2. The Witch Finder or the Executioner strips a destitute old woman and shaves her to locate private and small marks where the devil has sucked. Historian Sharpe claims that the stripping and washing becomes a way for the Interrogator to know a woman's body, to make it speak of what it has done, and it will not suffice.

Teat, Speak! [Bell]

3. The interrogator tortures to reveal the "mumbling language" of one familiar and the "hollow, sharp' voice" of another.

Familiar, Speak! [Bell]

4. It spoke English, moaned Alice Device in 1612. Doggie asked for her soul. In return, it would give her the power to do anything.

Familiar, suck! [Bell]

LISTENING EXERCISES

LISTENING EXERCISE I

Listen to the following paragraph
and answer the questions:

The canine as familiar is a spotted bitch, a rugged sandy dog coming in through the window, a black hound talking and standing up, a large brown poodle dog on his saddle...a thought-form who may vanish at will but also may drink from a private and small mark on the witch's body until the familiar has the strength to carry out a certain task on the astral plane.

Questions:

1. Is this passage from contemporary witchcraft manuals and historic legal documents?

2. Are the bodily differences amongst apparitions significant?

Listen to the following speech lovingly. Then, repeat it in your own words. But first, follow these commands:

Stand as if you inhabited a humane bosom.
Clear your throat.
Remember.
Make a mental list of the animated dogs of
your childhood.
Prepare to recite an ode to your canine familiar.
Now, listen lovingly.

Hurra! We've got them at last! The dogs are at them... dogs are intended to ferret out the Indians...let not a red nigger escape, show no mercy, exterminate them. We'll close the Florida War.

Caress the view of torn flesh.
We must erect a virile nation.

Don't collect their howls. Instead, rejoice. Sow the seeds of the Wolfowitz Doctrine. Seminoles will nurture his dogs, GB, ZK, AM, RP. Together they'll close the War.

Now, repeat in your own loving words.

Today, like many days ago, witch-finders and chasseurs learn to pacify beasts proliferating in the Empire by becoming familiar with domestication manuals. Listen to an excerpt of one such text and answer the following questions.

The dog must be kept chained.
A negro must be in the horizon.
His trainer must be desperate.
They must, at all times, be muzzled.
The dog must be beaten brutally. Literary.
The trainer must be hardy and brave.
Bitch must be scrupulously honest
  and remarkably faithful.
The dog must be starved. Must possess a machete.
They must, at all times, be muzzled.
A negro prize must be procured. Until
  his structure changes.
The dog must be beaten senseless. Or
  until his structure changes.
The bloody entrails of fellow beast must be procured.
The trainer must be scrupulously honest
  and remarkably faithful.
Bitch must be scrupulously honest
  and remarkably faithful.
The dog must have a negro.
President Zachary Taylor must have a negro bitch.

Question 1: How must the bitch use the machete?

Question 2: Who's the negro's familiar?

Question 3: What must you procure?

Question 4: Which bitch is the slave?

Question 5: Who is enhanced by this training?

Drawing on prior experience, please imitate/reproduce the following historically situated animal/human communications:

1. Pug forcing the pharyngeal gag reflex (rapid gasp snort):

(Recall Queen Victoria's fawn colored pug rapidly pulling in air through the nose, accompanied by an audible strange sound.)

Reverse sneeze, again:

2. Cuban bloodhound, trained to track and attack the slave/revolutionary snuffles:

(Dog's shallow graves could be found on plantations. In an act of witchery rebellion, field hands in Matthew Fontaine Maury's plantation killed six dogs out of a pack of twenty-five after they were unleashed to track their familiars who had made it to the woods of Spotsylvania County, Virginia. They buried them quietly in the cotton rows.)

Snuffle, loudly:

3. Chocolate Labrador Retriever woofing softly at a ball:

(Boris de Main was a yellow bitch born in 1920 that seemed to carry the chocolate gene and the mother of Diver of Chilton Foliat, the first liver-colored retriever registered by the AKC in 1932.)

Softly woof at fake bomb in drawer:

(Labrador Retrievers are regularly used in explosives detection work.)

4. Pretend you are your puppy's tale. Get tired tracing it.

(In the plantation, dogs loved chasing their tails. Sometimes, recalls a former maroon, "they called the hands from the field and made them run around the house and climb trees, with the dogs after them.")

Woof:

5. French Bull Dog vomiting from the strain of attempting to penetrate the female sexed.

(Due to breeding, the vulva is set too high and artificial insemination is recommended.)

Repeat gagging sound:

6. German Shepherd aggressively barking with intent to bite:

(Azit is the dog star of a 1970's IDF cult film that transforms the perception of the German Shepherd from Nazi guard dog to Israeli fighter attacking Arabs inside and outside of occupied territories. Azit appears to understand complex Hebrew commands but does not respond in Hebrew; the silence of a working dog is accompanied by jazzy flute.)

Bark accusatorially:

(The animal is believed to have been with his 59-year-old owner when she was found hanging from the ceiling of her Paris flat. The dog is led into the witness box by a vet to see how she reacts to a suspect. The stenographer is ordered to 'record all of the dog's barks.' Palais de Justice in Paris confirmed that the Nanterre case was the first time a dog had appeared as a witness in criminal proceedings in France.)

Bark furiously:

Questions about dogs as companion species by way of Donna Haraway:

To Donna, the dog/human alliance sutures human/creature divides and you don't agree and you agree...

Your fingers accidentally grazed the dog's genitals and her tongue once slid into your mouth and you regularly hold her hot shit in your palm and once in awhile the plastic bag has a small hole...transfection occurs. Genetic material is swapped to what end?

Silent response: In the swamp, declares Solomon Northup, there is no space for intra-species grazing of genitals or for the transfection of genetic material.

I staggered on, fearing every instant I should...be crushed within the jaws of some disturbed alligator. The dread of them now almost equalled the fear of the pursuing hounds.

If the transfection occurs...shreds of Frida Kahlo's human microbiome are carried in the charcoal-colored descendents of her own Xoloitzcuintli dogs...and not in opposite, Xolo dog in Kahlo progeny. Haraway describes her own reversal of condition: she, settler-human-philosopher reproductively silent by choice and her settler-Australian sheepdog undergoing "surgery without consultation."

QUESTION:

How does their transfection transfer into other consorting forms?

REPEAT:

Transfection
Companion Species
Intra-Action

Repeat the following sentences and spew out the words that don't belong:

Preaching is a mother who conceives and gives birth to faith. The twelve chosen women know what it is like to conceive, nourish, and give birth to a sermon.

Let's chart the impure genealogy of the pet and the contemporaneous delineation of the home as the uniquely private enclosure, where the *pater familias* rules over his own secluded world of domesticated property wife, children, servants, and animals.

A few wild species may have been unexpectedly domesticated by human architecture itself: Hans Zinsser speculates that the inexplicable disappearance of the Black Death after its epidemic levels through the seventeenth century may have to do with the "increased domestication." According to the author, the development of cellars, attics, food storage buildings kept rats "contentedly at home" where they could not spread disease with such efficiency.

Civil order is fragile without domestication. *Cogito, ergo sum* pivots on the vivification of the dog.

Is the sensual texture of Donna's consorting forms not a comforting dwelling for the anxious/erotic erasure of colonial impulses?

REPEAT:

A resemblance is here said to exist between rebellion and witchcraft.

Blueprints: Fitness

BLUEPRINTS FOR A PRESIDENTIAL YOUTH FITNESS TEST

NOVEMBER 2016

EXAMINATION GROUNDS

—

159 PIONEER STREET

BROOKLYN, NEW YORK

UNITED STATES

STATION 1
Sit And Reach To Milk That Sickly Slum Cow
[Flexibility] [You're A Loose One]

OBJECTIVE
To measure flexibility of lower back and hamstrings

A straight line two feet long is marked on the floor as the baseline.	*Indicate line. Indicate that this is the sickly slum cow.*
A measuring line four feet long is drawn perpendicular to the midpoint of the baseline.	*Indicate line again.* *Indicate that this marks where the milker finds her human body transecting cow body.* *Indicate that here sassafras, locust, poplar and cedar stands stood and stooped. Chopt.*
Extending two feet on each side and marked off in half-inches.	*Indicate that the cow is in a shantytown built with pilfered lumber on a low hill surrounded by salt marshes; circled by mills, factories, and distilleries.*
The point where the baseline and measuring line intersect is the "0" point.	*Speak: Just north is the whip factory, according to historic record, named Back's.* *Each whip finds home, hide, hole, nail to hang from.*
Student removes shoes and sits on floor with measuring line between legs and soles of feet placed immediately behind baseline, heels 8–12 inches apart.	*Someone feed the cow: factory slop, distillery mash.*

With hands on top of each other, palms down, the student places them on measuring line.	*Pronounce the year and month: April 1857.*
With the legs held flat by a partner, the student slowly reaches forward as far as possible, keeping fingers on the measuring line and feet flexed.	*Prompt student to strip the teat, disinfect the teat, and express until the udder is empty.*
After three practice tries, the student holds the fourth reach for three seconds while that distance is recorded.	*You con. Stretch the dupe.* *Deliver "pure country milk" to Brooklyn's rich.*

SCORING

Legs must remain straight, soles of feet against box, and fingertips of both hands should reach evenly along measuring line. Scores are recorded to the nearest centimeter.

STATION 2
Endurance/Climb
To Scale Home Mountain

OBJECTIVE
To measure heart/lung
endurance by fastest time
to cover a designated distance

Review health status.	*Let participant know the synthetic/bureaucratic Famine is bone-evident. No food over time equals structural damage.*
Times are recorded in minutes and seconds.	*Begin measuring their time at forty feet from the lip of the sidewalk to the top of the rocky top.*
Warm up.	*Start them at the bottom of the quarry thirty feet below but beside the lip of the sidewalk.*
Pace yourself as it is a one mile distance.	*Instruct: By way of winding, rickety staircases.*
Cover the distance in as short a time as possible.	*Subtract 130 years and add 6.3 miles.*
Begin running on the count, “Ready? Go!”	*Journalist: “Why is this...population permitted in the city?”*
Walking may be interspersed with running.	*Or squatting, squatters.*

Cool down.	*Prompt: class status is where you sleep.*

SCORING

Times are recorded in minutes and seconds.

STATION 3
Curl Ups
Slave-Automaton

OBJECTIVE
To measure abdominal strength/ endurance by maximum number of curl-ups performed in one minute.
To measure level of exertion.

Have student lie on cushioned, clean surface with knees exed and feet about 12 inches from buttocks.	*Indicate to slave-automaton: take 5 steps towards the line. Stop for 5 seconds. Begin again. Remind slave-automaton that the line seats in the horizon, across the Bay.*
Partner holds feet.	*Command: Utter the following words, silently:* *What is the USA principle?* *What does each letter stand for?*
Arms are crossed with hands placed on opposite shoulders and elbows held close to chest. *Additional instructions to achieve exertion*: The automaton must also cross her legs, the other holds feet firmly. With her arms extended at a 90 degree angle, she must write in the air, the answer to the question above.	*The USA principle is a common sense approach to automation and process improvement projects.* *Slave-automaton must utter:* *"U" means understand the existing process* *"S" stands for simplify the process* *"A" stands for automate the process.*

Keeping this arm and leg position, student raises the trunk, curling up to touch the outside of forearms and elbows to thighs and then lowers the back to the floor so that the scapulae (shoulder blades) touch the floor, for one curl-up.	*As the slave-automaton-worker raises her trunk, she must consort with her Irish other. She must repeat what the IO tells her.* *Slave-automaton-worker recites:* *P = time per cubic yard picking, loading, and wheeling any given kind of earth to any given distance when the wheeler loads his own barrow.* *T = Percentage of a day required to rest and necessary delays.* *S = Time dumping and turning.* *D = Time filling the shovel and straightening up ready to throw.*
To start, a timer calls out the signal, "Ready? Go!" and begins timing student for one minute.	*To start, the engine roars. The Irish other raises his trunk, curling down to touch the bottom of the salty marsh. Repeat action five times.*
The student stops on the word "stop."	*Whistle sounds.* *Let slave-Automaton-worker know that she can:* *Twitch toward motionless.*

SCORING

"Bouncing" off the floor is not permitted. The curl-up should be counted only if performed correctly.

STATION 4
Bone Structure Strength

OBJECTIVE
To measure body durability.
To place the student-automaton in the space of exception or in riot mode.
To excise banzo.

The student must position her body in the following manner: hands under shoulders, arms straight, fingers pointed forward, and legs straight, parallel, and slightly apart (approximately 2–4 inches) with the toes supporting the feet. Keeping the back and knees straight, the student then lowers the body until there is a 90-degree angle formed at the elbows with upper arms parallel to the floor.	*Advise the student that:* 1. *In the future she will commit suicide by eating bittersweet scraps of earth.* 2. *Banzo: The first mental disease produced by capital.* 3. *Mbanzo* 4. *Mbonzo* 5. *Dubium Mare (Stormy Sea)* 6. *Definitions belong to the definers, not the defined.*
Student must complete 1 push-up every 3 seconds. The push-ups are performed to a recording of drums.	*Intimate to the student that:* *"There is a loneliness that can be rocked. Arms crossed, knees drawn up, holding, holding on, this motion, unlike a ship's, smooths and contains the rocker. It's an inside kind—wrapped tight like skin. Then there is the loneliness that roams. No rocking can hold it down. It is alive. On its own. A dry and spreading thing that*

	makes the sound of one's own feet going seem to come from a far-off place." Beloved.
Student cannot rest. Movement must be continual until the drum or the metronome stops.	*We flesh; flesh that weeps* *Yonder they do not love your flesh* *They will see it broken and break it again* *Hear me: they do not love your neck unnoosed and straight.*

SCORING
Record only those push-ups done with proper form, completed in three seconds and in rhythm.

Possible drum score for Bone Structure Strength Exercise: Art Blakey's "Ya Ya," *Orgy in Rhythm* (1957).

Answer Keys

ARE: BEAUTIFUL ECONOMY
ANSWER KEY

1. (E)

2. (C)
   (The absence of grace) (Our graceless economy)

3. (B)

4. (E)

5. (D)

6. (D)

7. (A) or (C)
   (Although it would be excellent to make a case for (D) and (E).)

8. (E)
   (See Brian Holmes lecture at EGS that speaks of the economic devastation of the 1970's as a windfall for invention [liposuction; ethernet; liquid crystal display]. Technological Implementation of these innovations takes place in the 1980's, after the recession.)

9. (A) (C) (D) (E)

10. (A) (B) (C) (D) (E)

(All correct in ways both terrible and curious.)

11. Ⓐ Ⓑ Ⓒ Ⓔ
(A physicist was the son of a prison guard in the California system. After work, his father would give him the weapons he had confiscated. Crude shanks in small hands.)

12. Ⓐ Ⓒ Ⓓ Ⓔ

13. Ⓐ Ⓒ Ⓓ Ⓔ

14. Ⓔ

15. Ⓑ and Ⓔ

16. Ⓐ Ⓒ Ⓓ Ⓔ

17. Ⓐ Ⓒ Ⓓ Ⓔ

18. Ⓐ Ⓒ Ⓓ Ⓔ

19. Ⓐ Ⓑ and Ⓔ

20. Ⓐ Ⓒ Ⓓ Ⓔ

21. Ⓐ or Ⓔ

22. Ⓒ

23. Ⓐ Ⓒ Ⓓ Ⓔ

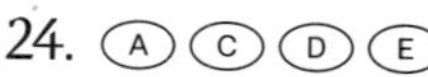

25. (A) (C) (D) (E)

26. (A) (C) (D) (E)

27. (A) or (D)

(It is true that the Mohawk word for vulva translates as “nice canoe” but Cook makes no correlation between the charm of the term and a cultural resistance to misogyny. This conflation belongs to the test-maker. The conflation is a situational conflagration: these words are sourced from the Smith College Oral History Archive. I made a composite of digital file and brick and mortar library full of women and books.

It is true that Cook does not claim that she is fighting misogyny. It is true that Cook is battling settlers’ poisons and settlers’ laws and settlers’ settling.

It is true that massaging a woman’s breasts increases the frequency of the contractions and that loving words dilate the cervix of a woman in labor, but Cook does not reference these aspects of natural delivery in her text. Ina May Gaskin, a Tennessee midwife and founder of The Farm, includes these details in her seminal book on midwifery. It is true that Gaskin and her followers are still settlers. Despite.)

28. (A) (C) (D) (E)

ARE: THE REPRODUCTIVE ANSWER KEY

Questions and Answers: Abraham Adams, Susan Briante, Kaye Cain-Nielsen & Judah Rubin, Desert Hearts, Rafael Kelman, Claire Lehmann, Farid Matuk, Mary Walling Blackburn. All uncredited answers are written by MWB.

1. Ⓐ Ⓑ Ⓒ Ⓓ Ⓔ
   Something must be at stake otherwise I am not sure why we gather, drink, quiet down, read and mark. Even now, can you open pinky / wet your thumb / sink down to a bad place / knock the fat clean out of your eye?

2. Ⓒ 1ʃ ɕɾʔ 1ʃ ʃɾc1ɾ)cʃ\
   This question is written in Shavian. Shavian is a new (1950) alfa-bet that aims to increase the speed of penmanship and restore the relationship between the sound and the mark. *What I see is how it sounds if I know what I* Ⓒ George Bernard Shaw, Irish playwright, funds the invention of a Shaw script. The man is "struck by the wastage in English spelling." He means that his hand houses its own factory; fingers inefficiently labor over silent letters and irregularities. A designer of alphabets will be awarded 500 pounds. Fluent Shavian writer makes fewer strokes per letter. It will take 3-4 hours to learn to read again to learn to read English in Shavian. After that it will be clear.

3. (A)

mek ə kapi

4. (E)

Start over (stutter). 1. The schoolyard is the grounds of ritual utterances...

4. (E)

Twig. Puppet. Beast. Clone. All and none.

5. (E)

Not a young thief. Not a young animal. Not carrion. Not infant. Yet the mother is robbed and holding the decaying flesh of her young one. It's a drawing by Kathe Kollwitz. It's a drawing by a metal head. It's our wartime; the suitcase with rollers is a coffin for a toddler (carry-on). I swap charcoal and marker for Vine. Online I vine the child, dead and alive. Horrible I loop the horror. Carry on.

6. (B)

Ghost fruit. [The ghost fruit is the manifestation of the completely recessive gene [gh]. But Gardeners and Gamers both verbally traffic in this metaphor of the colorless half-being. Ghost Stock. Ghost Seedling. The gardener is cautious of the unripe; the gamer feels fetal, close-circuited.]

7. (E)

Women is not WIF. A pre-wave feminist told us so.

8. Ⓔ
Sulfur : Car [*contributed by Susan Briante*]

9. Ⓒ
Apple : rare earth [*contributed by Rafael Kelman*]

10. Ⓐ Ⓑ Ⓓ
Ⓐ 21st century prisoners' abortion rights : Mothering from Inside
Ⓑ 19th century British Female Insane Asylum as Holding Tank for Unruly Middle Class Wives : control classroom for child dosages of ritalin administered to establish inhibitory control
Ⓓ Some of the above

11. Ⓓ
Consent : to not be a single being
or Ⓔ waves : waves
Possible write-in answer: Smudging one scream into another inches above the parking lot of Disneyland : child sex trafficking [*contributed by Farid Matuk*]

12. No answer is correct. [*contributed by Abraham Adams*]

13. All answers are correct. [*contributed by Desert Hearts*]
Ⓐ exorcism : family reunion
Ⓑ gesture : remote control
Ⓒ poetry : pyramid

(D) Alien : Predator
(E) Orgasm : Organism

14. (A) (C) (D)
(A) The gaze of the pedophile.
(C) the hole of the photograph.
(D) a robot's algorithm.

15. All answers are correct if Tester wants them to be. [They are auto-tuned].
Tester, please yourself.

16. (E) (B) and (C)
This question and answer set is derived from Dr. Robert Wyman's Yale Open-Course: Global Problems of Over/Population.

Tester, please note the class hierarchy inherent in the situation in answer (B) is not properly attended to by the question itself. [(B) *The act of an orangutan raping a human who served as the cook at a biologist's encampment.*] In the literary symbolic the orangutan assaults the leading scientist opposed to the lowest ranking member of the human crew. In my Marxist novella, the scientist gut cries to the university psychoanalyst about the violence of the subject. In Wyman's actual lecture to "Yalies," based on factual reportage, he notes that that the cook's husband asserts that "at least the cook was not raped by a human.' Is this because it is not reproductive? And what of the global violence of the Visitor Researcher (fresh inoculations; fresh drawers; fresh ballot? Tester. I can't stop testing you.) Examiner, it is an absentee ballot, yours and theirs.

17. (A)
    Screw, screw. [*contributed by Rafael Kelman*]

18. All and none are correct. [*contributed by Kaye Cain-Nielsen & Judah Rubin*]

19. All and none are correct. [*contributed by Kaye Cain-Nielsen & Judah Rubin*]

20. All and none are correct. [*contributed by Kaye Cain-Nielsen & Judah Rubin*]

21. (E)
    Represent a highly conservative strain of American patriarchy. [*contributed by Claire Lehmann*]

22. (A)
    Herald a new value system *and/or* (D) usher in societal liberation. [*contributed by Claire Lehmann*]

23. All answers are correct:
    Fearlessness Tenacity Stomach Intestinal Fortitude Indomitableness. [*contributed by Claire Lehmann*]

24. Select all possible answers. [*contributed by Kaye Cain-Nielsen & Judah Rubin*]

25. An Abortion Pop playlist knelled along pre-test. Scores of rock melodies announced the end of embryos, relationships, and reproductive freedoms and are overproduced by Pro-Choice and Anti-Choice ranks. Two (1971) songs were singled out for the examination essay section.

Tester, write to them and through them. Lee Hazlewood sings/describes his girlfriend's womb: *Dark is the canyon when life is beginning* while he unspools: the relation cannot withstand the termination of a pregnancy. *The knives that have touched you where others have touched you.*

Lorene Mann wrote and recorded "Hide My Sin" in Nashville after "seeing a sign advertising abortion information on a billboard in downtown Nashville." Chet Atkins accompanies on fiddle. A choral group spells out: A-B-O-R-T-I-O-N-I-N-N-E-W-Y-O-R-K. Tester writes through emotions sieved through kitsch. Kitsch, near to cheese, strains political structures. *Everyone's a Stranger/ There's no friend.*

26. All punctuation, extinct and common, is acceptable:

The weeping mark is the obelus—used for corrective deletions of invalid reconstructions: ÷

This is the effect even if Tester imagines a table with one orange on its surface and one orange on the floor below it. A horizon line for a liquid surface: a buoy bobbling, a body submerged.

Also, the hashtag/*libra pondo* is a gross response but it is the Tester's right to be snide and slick.

I won't love you for it but I, Examiner, also won't

even remember which Tester is whom, in the end.

The Examiner's Oath: to reverse the old nature of the exam; its long, fuckless fuck.

The Tester's Oath: to expand the nature of the measurement.

*The examinations are graded in Dallas, Texas.
To situate: When a child is arrested by the Dallas Police, after they are fingerprinted and booked, they are transported to the Henry Wade Juvenile Justice Center; Henry Wade served as the city's District Attorney (1951-1987) and was the named defendant in Roe vs. Wade.

To continue: In 2013, the HQ of the American Board of Obstetrics and Gynecology, located in Dallas, ruled that gynecologists could not treat men, although the anoscopy procedure gynecologists use to identify anal cancers is identical regardless of gender. After national pressure, the measure was reversed.

To elaborate: While grading examinations, local news breaks the sexual transmission of a high replicating Zika virus in Dallas. The transmitter, named Patient 0, is framed as traveler. If either end of the couple are bit by a local mosquito variant, *Aedes aegypti*, the virus will reproduce itself throughout the area.

To End: Les Cousins, the rusted French term for mosquitoes.
Me, Examiner am my disease. Me vector. We vector.

Results

Dear Tester #1:

You will insist on a number.

Here is your number: 1000

Essay #2: The semi-colon is a pause. This is a rigorous answer. Thank you. The examiner must pause. Madame Y., full-spectrum doula, is clear that she is operating within the pause between cadaver and soil. Tester pauses. How can this be tested?

Dear Tester #6:

Here is your number: 85

This is an extremely high score.

Notes on Essays: You communicate that there was some trouble following the choral group's spelling as it interlaced through the body of the song. Fair enough! Lorene Mann's single "Hide My Sin," employs a choral group to spell out A-B-O-R-T-I-O-N-I-N-N-E-W-Y-O-R-K. The ARE maintains that questions that arise in the test should not stay with the test but wheedle their way back to you, Tester.

Dear Tester #5:

Your score is useless because tests are useless.

Bubbled grids do not hold you or channel your abilities.

Essays under pressure crack and slash at the continuities you would trace and parse with time. Our results are *Queen*-haunted:

This is our last dance

This is ourselves

Under pressure

When I lived in Turkey, state administered examinations did not offer second chances; your score was your fate. When I lived in the US, capitalism allowed the capitalists to take the exam as many times as they could afford. This enabled the rich to sacrifice their childhoods to test preparation. The remaining children pooled in lesser conditions, stranger positions, less vertical movement.

Queen again.

It's the terror of knowing

What this world is about

We'd like a Queen-haunted testing structure; one that produces a terror in knowing. We asked you to take a test with us because we were operating under the construct that if there must be an examination administered en masse, we wanted to imagine together a test that might reflect the actual concerns of the people in the room. We wanted to create a test that eschews logic structures. This time we wanted a test that emphasized reproductive systems because they are ensnarled in the phallus.

Some of you will insist on a number.

Here is your number: 80

Note on Essay: It was a pleasure to read this line in your essay on Texan Lee Hazlewood: "*something inside <u>me</u> must not be denied <u>me</u>*—what a dick this guy is!" We thank you for knowing that emotion counts and we count it in your score. A further investigation of Hazlewood reveals a rather extended feature length music video: *A Cowboy in Sweden.* We are also still thinking about your description of the Houston anti-choice protesters as *honey-voiced* and their subsequent pitch shifts. We will continue to think of the sonic register of patriarchy as it faints in and out of cock rock, country lounge, and Pro-Life frontline.

"*Pay me reparations for your fucking sperm.*" We thank you for knowing that emotion counts and we count it in your score. Your righteous call for compensation is fused with humor when you incorporate Hazlewood's narcissistic chant of "me" into your response "*is my response to the man who wrote his first song for me.*"

The last line of your essay: "I don't trust the woman you hired" is opaque. Opaque is derived from *opacus*, Latin for "darkened." The line is darkened and then erased. The examiner fails your test.

Dear Tester #10:

Insist on a number.

Here is your number: 8 is considered holy in Japan. It is the perfection of a pair: an abstract pair, that is not human or other sentient beast. Two spheres in the hand.

Notes on Essays: "*God is sooo not there for the heteros/ haterrz.*" The blur in the spelling is a fecund thing for us. God has abandoned MAN, Mr. Nietzsche. But not woman lovers. You continue: "*He knowzz what shit is + he's like that shit is straight dumb.*" The shit of the abortion and the shit of those who deny the abortion. A He-God despite the he-ness between his mind/legs. You are hopeful, Tester. You end: *I love you.* We assume you offer us love. If this is so, we accept and return it. If you offer it to Lorene Mann, we confusedly turn to the side and let it flow towards her.

Dear Tester #7:

Your number: 60

60 is a harshad number, coined by Indian mathmatician D. R. Kaprekar. Harshad derives from Sanskrit and means joy-giver.

Notes on Essays: It was a pleasure to read this line in your essay on Texan Lee Hazlewood: "*and two of those hands will be me*—what a narcissist!" We thank you for knowing that emotion counts and we count it in your score. We understand why you elided Hazlewood with forced dentistry pop although we are forced to admit that when we were young we were electrified by lighter Hazlewood sleaze—a Nancy Sinatra duet. Sinatra reveals that it was very hard for her initially to write and perform a feminist anthem...that she "had to dig deep" in herself to locate her feminism. We suspect you are not fishing around inside yourself attempting to locate a womyn-ish bone.

Dear Tester #12:

Number: 9

Hesiod's anvil takes 9 days to travel through the cosmos to the earth. It takes nine days for Hesiod's anvil to travel from the Earth to Hell. Nine is the operative number for an ancient poet ensnared in "CAD rendering" a tool released from its purpose. The test has been released from the cultural purpose. We have nothing to admit you to but we'd like you to keep your thoughts in motion. Hesiod is devoted to motion, an anvil as a thought, 18 days in flight.

Notes on Essays: Tester, your essay was very finely wrought. Thank you.

The analysis of the Manne's "Hide My Sin" animates the song; one could liken it to a corpse that jerks with each electric observation. You have underscored *"a regime of visibility...a scoptic drive which determines morality."* The choral group in acrostic croon is replaced in our Examining Mind; a surveillance camera peeks out of blue choir gown, a headless being with an eye at the end of its neck stump. Thank you.

Ano

ANO, AN EXIT.
(OUR AFTERWORD)

11-11-2016

RIO DE JANEIRO / BROOKLYN, NY

We used to insist to ourselves that the government's touch was so light—we hardly felt it! Night swim; grog; grinding beat; clitoris in a mouth; books stained by eating while reading—this was at center: but still gridded by a mechanical relationship to citizenship that kept us out of jail. We libertines felt that pleasure was the political work; we could eschew rules, meetings, examinations made by middle-class henchmen—and that then, perhaps eventually the false structure would wither or forget us.

Government bored us.

Still we took the government tests; lined up for government cheese and government shots in the ass; our paperwork foundered in dead cubicles. Bureaucrats gorged on our time. But Government was naturalized—as if it were sky and air and light. When we were finally grown females, the Government exposed itself as something that trafficked in Terror. Time passed.

Terror became boring.

It was naturalized—as regular as clocks, escalators, and tolls. Schools were also natural as detention centers. Tests were also natural as checkpoints. Naturally, tests nested in schools nested in Government. Prisoners nested in Detention Centers nested in natural Government.

To test is a form of government. To govern is to disseminate deleterious affects. Government puts the armature in place. Testing gives birth to the subject/

matter. This is the kind of government that does not permit outlying matter. The desire of government in the twenty-first century: to operate with pure impunity; to open the floodgates; to release all *others* into agony. The constant production of agony and profit. Nothing new here.

Except, in this global era, the magnate negates everything except whiteness and liquidity. Liquid capital: liquefaction of all *others*. Liquid terror, solidified anxiety and fear.

Because for so long we have depended on tests, we forgot that they made us liquid subjects. That is why we agreed to participate in this project. This is why we wanted to disrupt the logic of the GRE, the fitness test. Because we need to become solid again. No! Shapeshifters we cannot be. We cannot be because governments and governance is about making us lose our shape. Because the terror of the actuality of government is to convince that we must march, obey the clock and tolls, take the exam, obey the president. The day we write is the third day after Donald Trump was elected to be the incoming President of the United States of America.

Why pervert the test form/content at this historical juncture? To answer this question we think we must go back to the very real material uses of the test for the cumulus of acts of governance. The test binds corporeal arrangements into gendered holes, raging lunatics, white skins and black masks. The interruption of this binding process requires that we skew the test and its formal structures. This bending, this alteration, it is hoped, will shake the process of being subject and will introduce a bouncing question, a question that lingers, a perturbed state of being. A question that stringed together with other questions may resist one instance of governance.

The problem with tests is that they have the capacity of multiplying those who are not permitted to live within the boundaries of what we call society. This multiplying effect is the effect that we most fear. Multiplication and subtraction are the main operations of the test. Subtraction is embedded in the will to power. The test is naturalized and sutures subtracting and multiplying.

We believe that the will to power has always been obscene. But obscenity shapeshifts into different forms of life. As of now, the only tool we possess to undo obscenity, to obstruct it, to bend it, is a critical form of living. But criticism in the face of Trump obscenity is a form of suicide. And suicide right now does not act as political and it is not, as we think Lacan once said, the only ethical act. But then again, politics was sunk with the Zong. The only thing left is hatred and demagoguery. And we are unable to nuance either one. There is no safe ground, no safe sea, no safe boundary.

Safety is liquid.

Testing is just another dry tool that naturalizes the state's collusion with capitalism and racism. We refuse this. We turn their tools back on themselves, with pleasure. As surplus humans, the both of us, at the end of the Capitolocene, the test is also our surplus gesture. It is not our singular hopeless and hopeful act: this year we plant trees that will not reach their optimum height and we zombee fuck outside of species just to embed our genes in something—an End Times parlour trick...not unlike the last Maine wolf, circa 1908, fucking the coyote in half-logged dusk; the pelt of the mixed progeny is held at the L.C. Bates Museum on the grounds of an abandoned orphanage in Hinckley, Maine. But these pelts and tests, unmarked, are not active poems. They need some thing. Testers as strange pollinators, carrion beetles to the amorphophallus.

If our testers indeed moonlight as carrion beetles, they will bury themselves in the corpses of this epoch, emerging full, and alive even, with luck. We always wrote against regime and without instruction. We aren't *We*.

The following is a list of dates and locations where Anhoek pedagogical experiments, including the Record Examinations, were administered.

June 4–October 2, 2010
ANHOEK SCHOOL: RADICAL CITIZENSHIP: THE TUTORIALS.
At Governor's Island with No Longer Empty. New York City, NY.

September 17, 2010
ANHOEK SCHOOL: RADICAL CITIZENSHIP: THE TUTORIALS.
At Angel Island with Southern Exposure. San Francisco, CA.

January 28–29, 2011
ANHOEK SCHOOL: RADICAL CITIZENSHIP: THE TUTORIALS
I know you know I know you know I know, at Times Square Gallery. New York City, NY.

February 18, 2012
ANHOEK RECORDED EXAMINATION:
Beautiful Economy
Experience Economies. The Laboratory at Harvard University. Cambridge, MA.

April 28, 2014
ANHOEK SCHOOL WORKSHOP: FEMININE MARK /SLASH/Feminist Mark

Skowhegan and Intermedia MFA at University of Maine. Orono, ME.

June 6–July 3, 2014
ANHOEK SCHOOL: WMYN RADIO AND COFFEEHOUSE
Failure to Levitate. Elizabeth Foundation for the Arts. New York City, NY.

December 15, 2016
ANHOEK RECORDED EXAMINATION: THE REPRODUCTIVE
Cottage Industry. Booklyn and Sunview Luncheonette. Brooklyn, NY.

April, 3–June 25 2016
ANHOEK LISTENING LAB: (DOGGY) MOUTH OF (DOGGY) TRUTH
Shifters. Art in General. Brooklyn, NY.

November 19, 2016
ANHOEK ADULT PRESIDENTIAL FITNESS EXAM (TEST-RUN)
The Alternative Art School Fair. Pioneer Works. Brooklyn, NY.

November 3–December 2, 2016
ANHOEK LISTENING LAB: (DOGGY) MOUTH OF (DOGGY) TRUTH
Valegro. Slide Space 123. Oakland, CA.

BEAUTIFUL ECONOMY

1.	Ⓐ	Ⓑ	Ⓒ	Ⓓ	Ⓔ	Ⓕ	Ⓖ	Ⓗ	Ⓘ	___
2.	Ⓐ	Ⓑ	Ⓒ	Ⓓ	Ⓔ	Ⓕ	Ⓖ	Ⓗ	Ⓘ	___
3.	Ⓐ	Ⓑ	Ⓒ	Ⓓ	Ⓔ	Ⓕ	Ⓖ	Ⓗ	Ⓘ	___
4.	Ⓐ	Ⓑ	Ⓒ	Ⓓ	Ⓔ	Ⓕ	Ⓖ	Ⓗ	Ⓘ	___
5.	Ⓐ	Ⓑ	Ⓒ	Ⓓ	Ⓔ	Ⓕ	Ⓖ	Ⓗ	Ⓘ	___
6.	Ⓐ	Ⓑ	Ⓒ	Ⓓ	Ⓔ	Ⓕ	Ⓖ	Ⓗ	Ⓘ	___
7.	Ⓐ	Ⓑ	Ⓒ	Ⓓ	Ⓔ	Ⓕ	Ⓖ	Ⓗ	Ⓘ	___
8.	Ⓐ	Ⓑ	Ⓒ	Ⓓ	Ⓔ	Ⓕ	Ⓖ	Ⓗ	Ⓘ	___
9.	Ⓐ	Ⓑ	Ⓒ	Ⓓ	Ⓔ	Ⓕ	Ⓖ	Ⓗ	Ⓘ	___
10.	Ⓐ	Ⓑ	Ⓒ	Ⓓ	Ⓔ	Ⓕ	Ⓖ	Ⓗ	Ⓘ	___
11.	Ⓐ	Ⓑ	Ⓒ	Ⓓ	Ⓔ	Ⓕ	Ⓖ	Ⓗ	Ⓘ	___
12.	Ⓐ	Ⓑ	Ⓒ	Ⓓ	Ⓔ	Ⓕ	Ⓖ	Ⓗ	Ⓘ	___
13.	Ⓐ	Ⓑ	Ⓒ	Ⓓ	Ⓔ	Ⓕ	Ⓖ	Ⓗ	Ⓘ	___
14.	Ⓐ	Ⓑ	Ⓒ	Ⓓ	Ⓔ	Ⓕ	Ⓖ	Ⓗ	Ⓘ	___
15.	Ⓐ	Ⓑ	Ⓒ	Ⓓ	Ⓔ	Ⓕ	Ⓖ	Ⓗ	Ⓘ	___
16.	Ⓐ	Ⓑ	Ⓒ	Ⓓ	Ⓔ	Ⓕ	Ⓖ	Ⓗ	Ⓘ	___
17.	Ⓐ	Ⓑ	Ⓒ	Ⓓ	Ⓔ	Ⓕ	Ⓖ	Ⓗ	Ⓘ	___
18.	Ⓐ	Ⓑ	Ⓒ	Ⓓ	Ⓔ	Ⓕ	Ⓖ	Ⓗ	Ⓘ	___
19.	Ⓐ	Ⓑ	Ⓒ	Ⓓ	Ⓔ	Ⓕ	Ⓖ	Ⓗ	Ⓘ	___
20.	Ⓐ	Ⓑ	Ⓒ	Ⓓ	Ⓔ	Ⓕ	Ⓖ	Ⓗ	Ⓘ	___
21.	Ⓐ	Ⓑ	Ⓒ	Ⓓ	Ⓔ	Ⓕ	Ⓖ	Ⓗ	Ⓘ	___
22.	Ⓐ	Ⓑ	Ⓒ	Ⓓ	Ⓔ	Ⓕ	Ⓖ	Ⓗ	Ⓘ	___
23.	Ⓐ	Ⓑ	Ⓒ	Ⓓ	Ⓔ	Ⓕ	Ⓖ	Ⓗ	Ⓘ	___
24.	Ⓐ	Ⓑ	Ⓒ	Ⓓ	Ⓔ	Ⓕ	Ⓖ	Ⓗ	Ⓘ	___
25.	Ⓐ	Ⓑ	Ⓒ	Ⓓ	Ⓔ	Ⓕ	Ⓖ	Ⓗ	Ⓘ	___
26.	Ⓐ	Ⓑ	Ⓒ	Ⓓ	Ⓔ	Ⓕ	Ⓖ	Ⓗ	Ⓘ	___
27.	Ⓐ	Ⓑ	Ⓒ	Ⓓ	Ⓔ	Ⓕ	Ⓖ	Ⓗ	Ⓘ	___
28.	Ⓐ	Ⓑ	Ⓒ	Ⓓ	Ⓔ	Ⓕ	Ⓖ	Ⓗ	Ⓘ	___

1. Ⓐ Ⓑ Ⓒ Ⓓ Ⓔ Ⓕ Ⓖ Ⓗ Ⓘ ___
2. Ⓐ Ⓑ Ⓒ Ⓓ Ⓔ Ⓕ Ⓖ Ⓗ Ⓘ ___
3. Ⓐ Ⓑ Ⓒ Ⓓ Ⓔ Ⓕ Ⓖ Ⓗ Ⓘ ___
4. Ⓐ Ⓑ Ⓒ Ⓓ Ⓔ Ⓕ Ⓖ Ⓗ Ⓘ ___
4. Ⓐ Ⓑ Ⓒ Ⓓ Ⓔ Ⓕ Ⓖ Ⓗ Ⓘ ___
5. Ⓐ Ⓑ Ⓒ Ⓓ Ⓔ Ⓕ Ⓖ Ⓗ Ⓘ ___
6. Ⓐ Ⓑ Ⓒ Ⓓ Ⓔ Ⓕ Ⓖ Ⓗ Ⓘ ___
7. Ⓐ Ⓑ Ⓒ Ⓓ Ⓔ Ⓕ Ⓖ Ⓗ Ⓘ ___
8. Ⓐ Ⓑ Ⓒ Ⓓ Ⓔ Ⓕ Ⓖ Ⓗ Ⓘ ___
9. Ⓐ Ⓑ Ⓒ Ⓓ Ⓔ Ⓕ Ⓖ Ⓗ Ⓘ ___
10. Ⓐ Ⓑ Ⓒ Ⓓ Ⓔ Ⓕ Ⓖ Ⓗ Ⓘ ___
11. Ⓐ Ⓑ Ⓒ Ⓓ Ⓔ Ⓕ Ⓖ Ⓗ Ⓘ ___
12. Ⓐ Ⓑ Ⓒ Ⓓ Ⓔ Ⓕ Ⓖ Ⓗ Ⓘ ___
13. Ⓐ Ⓑ Ⓒ Ⓓ Ⓔ Ⓕ Ⓖ Ⓗ Ⓘ ___
14. Ⓐ Ⓑ Ⓒ Ⓓ Ⓔ Ⓕ Ⓖ Ⓗ Ⓘ ___
15. Ⓐ Ⓑ Ⓒ Ⓓ Ⓔ Ⓕ Ⓖ Ⓗ Ⓘ ___
16. Ⓐ Ⓑ Ⓒ Ⓓ Ⓔ Ⓕ Ⓖ Ⓗ Ⓘ ___
17. Ⓐ Ⓑ Ⓒ Ⓓ Ⓔ Ⓕ Ⓖ Ⓗ Ⓘ ___
18. Ⓐ Ⓑ Ⓒ Ⓓ Ⓔ Ⓕ Ⓖ Ⓗ Ⓘ ___
19. Ⓐ Ⓑ Ⓒ Ⓓ Ⓔ Ⓕ Ⓖ Ⓗ Ⓘ ___
20. Ⓐ Ⓑ Ⓒ Ⓓ Ⓔ Ⓕ Ⓖ Ⓗ Ⓘ ___
21. Ⓐ Ⓑ Ⓒ Ⓓ Ⓔ Ⓕ Ⓖ Ⓗ Ⓘ ___
22. Ⓐ Ⓑ Ⓒ Ⓓ Ⓔ Ⓕ Ⓖ Ⓗ Ⓘ ___
23. Ⓐ Ⓑ Ⓒ Ⓓ Ⓔ Ⓕ Ⓖ Ⓗ Ⓘ ___
24. Ⓐ Ⓑ Ⓒ Ⓓ Ⓔ Ⓕ Ⓖ Ⓗ Ⓘ ___

Quaestiones Perversas

First Printing
January 2017

Edition 1000

Pioneer Works Press
159 Pioneer St.
Brooklyn, NY 11231
pioneerworks.org

Pioneer Works is a center for research and experimentation in contemporary culture. Through a broad range of educational programs, performances, arts and science residencies, and exhibitions, Pioneer Works seeks to transcend traditional disciplinary boundaries, foster community, and provide a space where alternative modes of thought are supported and activated in tangible ways. Pioneer Works is a non-profit 501(c)(3).

Pioneer Works programs are made possible by the generous support of our board of directors, grants, and donations.

Quaestiones Perversas
is part of the
Groundworks Series

Editors
Catherine Despont
Zach White

Design
Daniel Kent

Copy Editor
Katie Giritlian

Typefaces
Gt Sectra
Dia

Paper
Rolland Enviro 100

Cover
Chipboard

ISBN
978-1-945711-03-9

Printed in Canada

Images from *Our World*. Manzanar High School Yearbook, 1944. Yearbook produced through the Manzanar Cooperative Enterprises under the War Relocation Authority. Scans provided by Beinecke Rare Book and Manuscript Library, Yale University. Photography copyright of Alan Miyatake, Toyo Miyatake Studio.

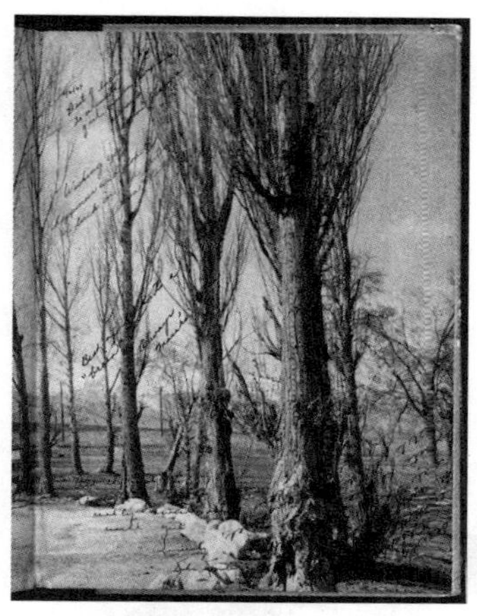

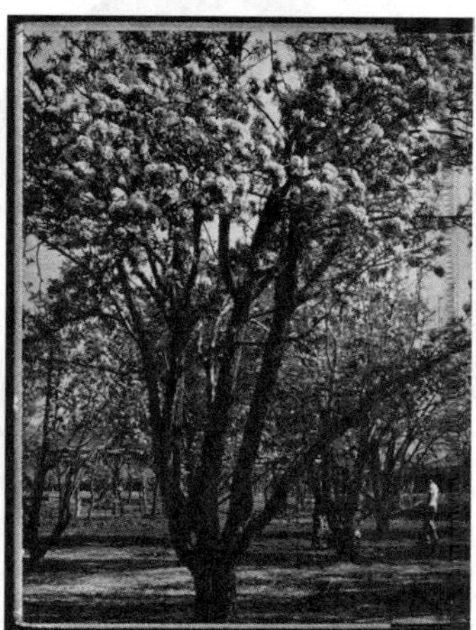

Inside flap images replicate Manzanar High School Yearbook endpapers, distributed to students imprisoned within the Manzanar Japanese-American Concentration Camp. Inscriptions to *Kiyoko, Kyoko, Kiyo-Chan, Kyo-Chan, or Katie* are written across the two images of the wooded creek. Beyond the creek, an arid encampment was rung by barbed wire. The same yearbook includes prohibited images (guard tower; hand with pliers poised to clip through the fence).

Photographer Toyo Miyatake, whose studies and exhibition history are entangled with Edward Weston, first made pictures disguising his homemade camera as a lunch pail.

Later: Miyatake allowed to make photographs if caucasian assistants (white wives of camp employees) snap shutter. Later: Miyatake permitted to independently operate camera. Later: Manzanar's director pens letter to graduating high school students photographed by Miyatake: NEVER WAS YOUR FUTURE AS BRIGHT AS NOW. Still 1944.

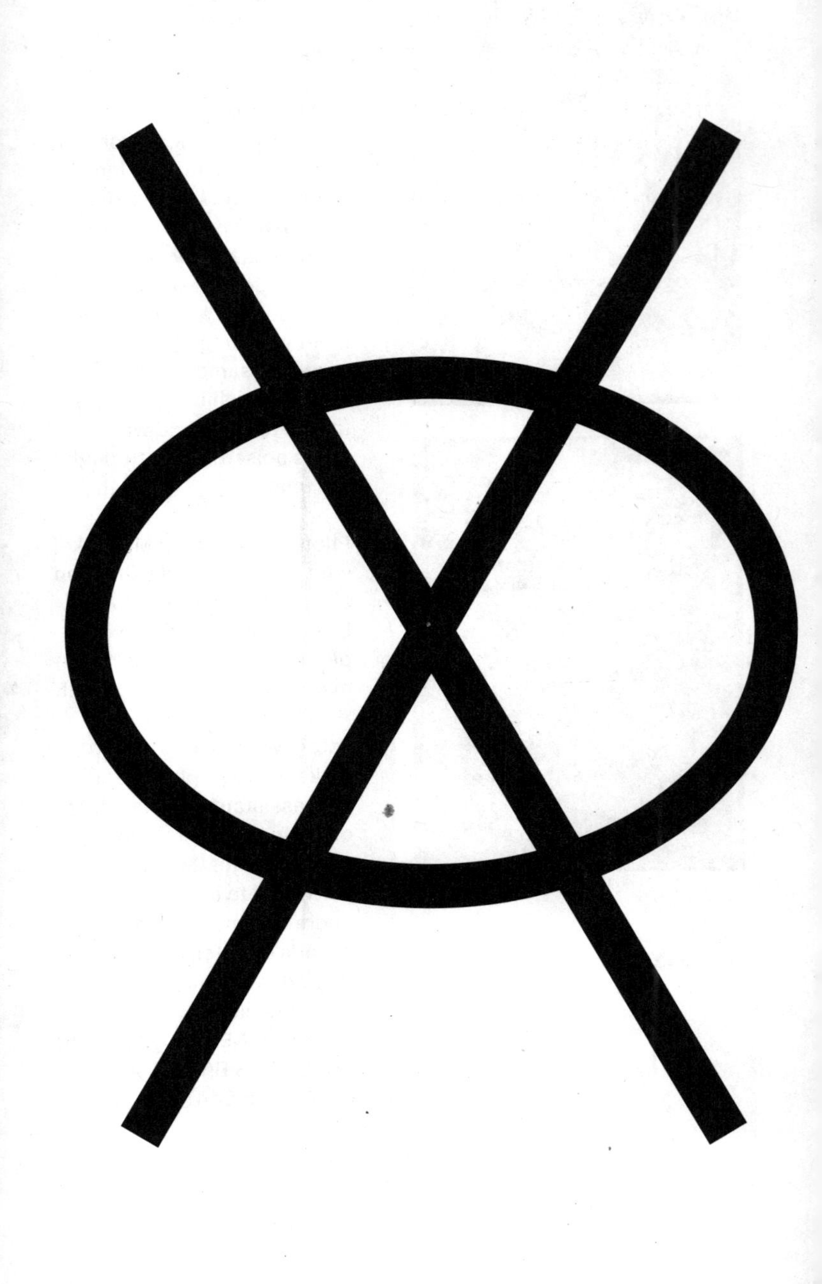